Amazing Histories

THE AMAZING HISTORY OF
MEDICINE

BY HEATHER MURPHY CAPPS

CAPSTONE PRESS
a capstone imprint

Published by Capstone Press, an imprint of Capstone.
1710 Roe Crest Drive, North Mankato, Minnesota 56003
capstonepub.com

Library of Congress Cataloging-in-Publication Data is available on the Library of Congress website.
ISBN: 9781669012047 (hardcover)
ISBN: 9781669011996 (paperback)
ISBN: 9781669012009 (ebook PDF)

Summary: Going to the doctor today looks a lot different than it did in the past. In fact, the entire history of medicine is riddled with unusual, amazing, and sometimes strange facts. Learn about how people used inventions, treatments, and more to survive and thrive in everyday life.

Editorial Credits
Editor: Alison Deering; Designer: Jaime Willems; Media Researcher: Jo Miller;
Production Specialist: Tori Abraham

Image Credits
Alamy: Hamza Khan, 19, Pictorial Press Ltd, 23 top, Science History Images, 8, 11, 15, 17, 18, 21; Getty Images: ilbusca, 24-25; Shutterstock: apichart sripa, 6, Daniel Chetroni, 29, Emilio100, 7, Everett Collection, cover, 1, left and right, back cover top left, New Africa, 9, Peakstock, 13, 27, peterfactors, cover top left, 30, Prostock-studio, back cover middle left, 5, Shutter_M, 10, Stock 4you, cover, 1 middle, Wikimedia: National Library of Medicine, 23 bottom

Printed and bound in the USA. PO 5195

TABLE OF CONTENTS

THE DOCTOR WILL SEE YOU NOW 4

EARLY MEDICINE 6

ANCIENT ADVANCES 10

FINDING BALANCE 14

OLD-SCHOOL SURGERIES 18

MEDICAL FIRSTS 22

PANDEMICS AND VACCINES 28

GLOSSARY 30

READ MORE 31

INTERNET SITES 31

INDEX 32

ABOUT THE AUTHOR 32

Words in **BOLD** are in the glossary.

THE DOCTOR WILL
SEE YOU NOW

No one likes to get sick. It was even worse in ancient times. People tried some pretty strange cures. Let's look at the amazingly gross history of medicine.

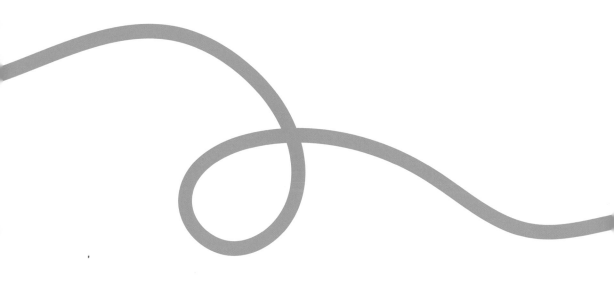

EARLY
MEDICINE

Nobody is sure when medicine first started. Ancient people didn't keep written records. They also didn't go to medical school. They often thought angry gods made people sick.

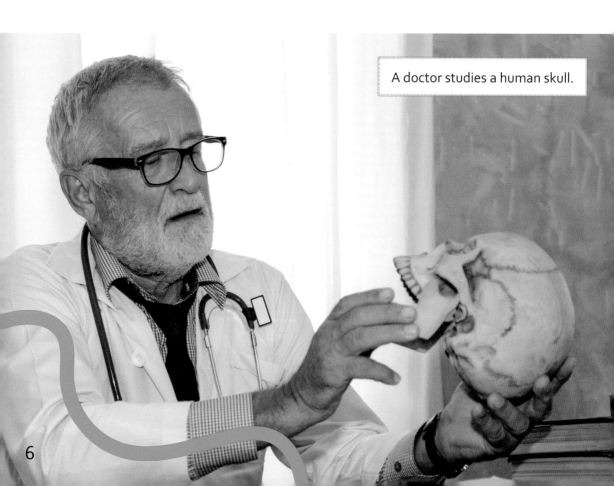

A doctor studies a human skull.

Healers used natural cures. People chewed

plants, such as yarrow, to help stomachaches.

Ayurveda

Doctors created **Ayurveda** more than 3,000 years ago. The word means "knowledge of life." This natural system of health started in India. It is still used today.

An Ayurvedic doctor takes a patient's pulse.

Doctors encourage good health. They tell people to exercise and eat a balanced diet. People also use foods such as garlic and ginger. These help people stay healthy.

ANCIENT
ADVANCES

Doctors in ancient Egypt made a special tea. They used willow tree bark and leaves. The tea helped headaches, sore muscles, and fevers. Honey was used on wounds. It killed germs.

Egyptian doctors wrote down their methods. These are some of our first medical records.

Ancient Egyptian medicine is some of the oldest in the world.

Acupuncture

In ancient China, doctors used **acupuncture.** They stuck tiny needles in different parts of the body. They even put needles in people's faces or ears. Ouch!

The needles seem to help. Some doctors still use them today. They say this method unblocks stuck energy. It helps fix headaches, sore muscles, and some sicknesses.

FINDING
BALANCE

Ancient Greek medicine was called **humorism**. But doctors weren't laughing. They believed people had fluids called humors. These included blood, yellow **bile,** black bile, and **phlegm.**

The Greeks believed these fluids had to be balanced. They tried to help people in some gross ways. They made people throw up or have diarrhea. Yuck!

DID YOU KNOW?

Hippocrates is known as the father of modern medicine. The Hippocratic oath, versions of which many medical schools still use, is named after him.

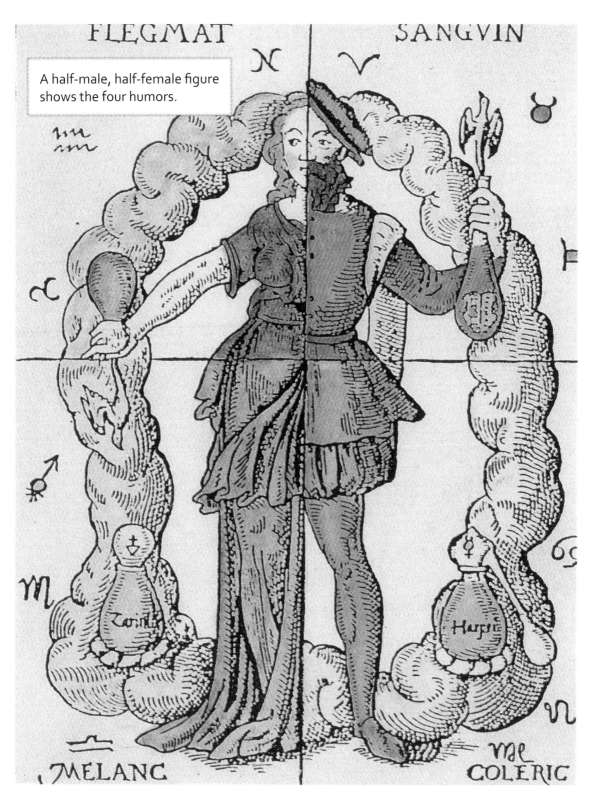

A half-male, half-female figure shows the four humors.

Bloodletting

Some ancient doctors also used bloodletting. They cut a person's veins to drain blood. They thought this helped with balancing the humors.

This process was dangerous. In 1685, King Charles II of England had a stroke. Doctors drained nearly 6 cups (3 pints) of his blood. The king died.

DID YOU KNOW?

George Washington, the first president of the United States, also died after bloodletting. Doctors drained nearly 40 percent of his blood.

Medieval artwork shows bloodletting being done.

OLD-SCHOOL
SURGERIES

One of the oldest known surgeries is a type of brain surgery. It was first done nearly 8,000 years ago. Doctors drilled a small hole into a person's skull. Yikes! They thought this could fix headaches, mental illness, and more.

A scene shows brain surgery being done in the 1500s.

An human skull shows evidence of brain surgery.

Plastic Surgery

Plastic surgery isn't new. The first nose job was done in India in 600 BCE.

Back then, criminals sometimes had their noses cut off. An Indian doctor learned how to help these people. He used skin from a cheek to make new noses.

A scene shows surgery in ancient India (800 BCE).

MEDICAL
FIRSTS

Italy's School of Salerno was the first medical school. It taught doctors from all over Europe. It was the first school to allow women to study and teach medicine.

Trotula was a doctor and teacher at the school. She wrote an important book on women's health. Some of her teachings are still used today.

A medieval medical school in Salerno, Italy

DID YOU KNOW?

Elizabeth Blackwell was the first woman to attend medical school in the United States. She graduated from New York's Geneva Medical College in 1850.

Human Dissection

Doctors didn't always know a lot about the human body. They first studied the bodies of animals to learn. But that led to *a lot* of wrong information. In the 1300s, studying dead human bodies was allowed.

But most people didn't want doctors to cut up dead relatives. Grave robbers dug up bodies instead. They sold the dead to medical schools.

Laughing Gas

Controlling pain during surgery wasn't always possible. But in the mid 1800s, doctors tried something new. They used **nitrous oxide**. This is also called laughing gas. People felt no pain after breathing this. Doctors could perform more surgeries.

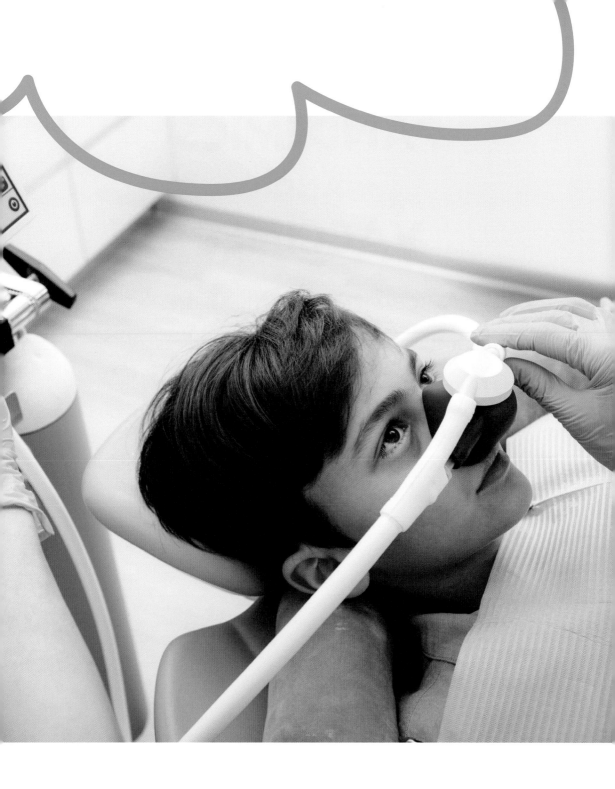

PANDEMICS
AND
VACCINES

In 430 BCE, a **plague** hit Athens, Greece. It was history's first **pandemic**. The disease was caused by bacteria spread by fleas and lice.

DID YOU KNOW?

During the Great Plague of London, doctors told people to breathe in smelly farts for protection. They believed it could keep people from getting sick.

Antibiotic medicines were created in the 1930s. They treated infections. Today, **vaccines** protect us against many diseases. These include measles, smallpox, and more. Hooray for modern medicine!

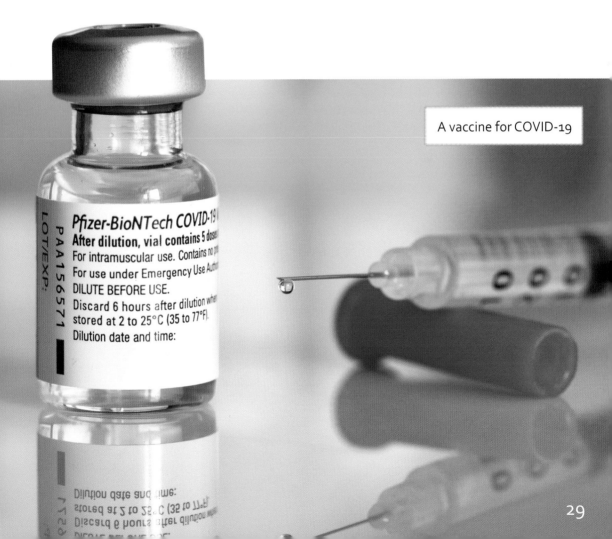

A vaccine for COVID-19

GLOSSARY

acupuncture (AK-yoo-puhngk-cher)—the stimulation of certain points in the body by penetrating the skin with metal needles

antibiotic (an-ti-bye-OT-ik)—a drug that kills bacteria and is used to cure infections and disease

Ayurveda (AH-yer-vey-duh)—an ancient Indian system of medicine

bile (BILE)— a green liquid that is made by the liver and helps digest food

humorism (HYOO-mer-iz-uhm)—outdated Greek theory of medicine that is based on balancing four bodily fluids

nitrous oxide (NEYE-truhss OK-side)—a gas made up of nitrogen and oxygen used to kill pain during surgery; also called "laughing gas"

pandemic (pan-DEM-ik)—a disease that spreads over a wide area and affects many people

phlegm (FLEM)— the thick snot that is produced when someone has a cold

plague (PLAYG)—a disease that spreads quickly and kills most people who catch it

vaccine (vak-SEEN)—a medicine that prevents a disease

READ MORE

Arnold, Nick. *Do No Harm: A Painful History of Medicine*. London: Welbeck Children's Books, 2021.

Messner, Kate. *History Smashers: Plagues and Pandemics*. New York: Random House Children's Books, 2021.

Parker, Steve. *Medicine: The Definitive Illustrated History*. New York: DK Publishing, 2016.

INTERNET SITES

Fact Monster: Medicine
factmonster.com/encyclopedia/medicine/general/terms/medicine/history-of-medicine

History for Kids
historyforkids.net

Know It All: History of Medicine: Kids Work!
knowitall.org/document/history-medicine-kids-work

INDEX

acupuncture, 12
antibiotics, 29
Ayurveda, 8–9

Blackwell, Elizabeth, 23
bloodletting, 16, 17

China, 12
Egypt, 10
exercise, 9

grave robbers, 25
Greece, 28

human dissection, 24–25
humorism, 14
humors, 14, 15, 16

India, 8, 20, 21

King Charles II, 16

medical records, 6, 10
medical schools, 6, 14, 22, 23

natural cures, 7, 9, 10
nitrous oxide, 26

pandemics, 28

sicknesses, 7, 10, 12, 18, 28–29

surgeries, 18, 19, 20, 26

vaccines, 29

ABOUT THE AUTHOR

photo credit: Jody McKitrick

Heather Murphy Capps grew up in a small Minnesota town where the motto is, "Cows, Colleges, and Contentment." She spent 20 years as a television news journalist before deciding to focus on her favorite kind of writing: books for kids involving history, social justice, science, magic, and a touch of mystery. She's a mixed-race author committed to diversity in publishing, an administrator/contributor to the blog From the Mixed-Up Files . . . of Middle-Grade Authors, and the author of the middle grade novel *Indigo and Ida* (Lerner/Carolrhoda Lab). Heather now lives in northern Virginia with her husband, two kids, and two cats.